Searchlight
BOOKS™

What Can We Learn from Early Civilizations?

Tools and Treasures of

# Ancient Egypt

Matt Doeden

Lerner Publications Company
Minneapolis

Lerner Publications Company
A division of Lerner Publishing Group, Inc.
241 First Avenue North
Minneapolis, MN 55401 U.S.A.

For reading levels and more information, look up this title at www.lernerbooks.com.


Library of Congress Cataloging-in-Publication Data

Doeden, Matt.
    Tools and treasures of ancient Egypt / by Matt Doeden.
        pages    cm. — (Searchlight books™—what can we learn from early
    civilizations?)
    Includes index.
    ISBN 978-1-4677-1429-7 (lib. bdg. : alk. paper)
    ISBN 978-1-4677-2505-7 (eBook)
    1. Egypt—Civilization—Juvenile literature.  2. Egypt—Social life and customs—
Juvenile literature.  3. Egypt—Antiquities—Juvenile literature.  I. Title.
DT61.D64 2014
932'.01—dc23                                                    2013015642

Manufactured in the United States of America
1 — PC — 12/31/13

# Contents

# Chapter 1

# THE ANCIENT EGYPTIANS

About five thousand years ago, the great civilization of ancient Egypt was growing. The lands of Upper Egypt and Lower Egypt joined to form one of the longest-lasting civilizations in history. This society flourished along the Nile River in northeastern Africa for thousands of years.

These Egyptian pyramids are more than four thousand years old. What else did the ancient Egyptians build?

The ancient Egyptians were skilled farmers and builders. They enjoyed art, music, and writing. They built pyramids and monuments. The bodies of many wealthy Egyptians were preserved by mummification. Mummies thousands of years old remain in good condition to this day!

**Egyptian artwork often told stories of day-to-day life. This painting shows people fishing.**

## Civilization in the Desert

Egypt has a harsh desert climate. It's hot. Little rain falls there. That's why the Egyptians settled along the Nile. The river provided them with almost everything they needed. It flooded every year.

The Nile River flowed through ancient Egypt. People depended on the Nile for water and food.

The floods covered the river's banks with rich soil. The Egyptians grew crops such as wheat and barley in this soil. They used the Nile's water to irrigate the crops. They caught fish from its waters.

The Egyptians believed that Hapi, the god of the Nile (ABOVE), gave them water for a good harvest.

The desert that surrounded Egypt also shaped the civilization. It left Egypt isolated from the rest of the world. Few invading armies dared to cross it. Egypt had little contact with other societies. That allowed Egypt to develop a culture like no other.

**The Egyptians called this vast desert the red land. The fertile soil around the Nile was called black land.**

# Ancient Egypt

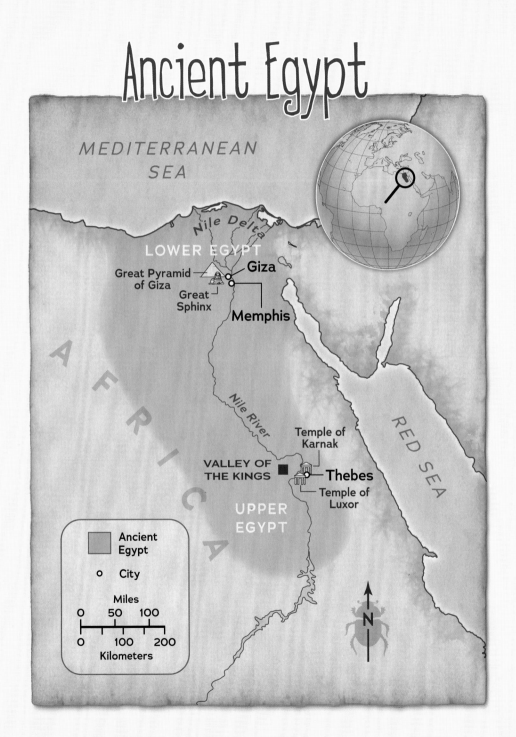

MEDITERRANEAN SEA

Nile Delta

LOWER EGYPT

Great Pyramid of Giza

Giza

Great Sphinx

Memphis

AFRICA

Nile River

Temple of Karnak

VALLEY OF THE KINGS

Thebes

Temple of Luxor

UPPER EGYPT

RED SEA

Ancient Egypt

○ City

Miles
0    50    100

0    100    200
Kilometers

N

# Chapter 2

# DAILY LIFE

Egyptians worked hard
to keep their society
strong.  They farmed.
They built tombs and temples.
Each person had a role.

Egyptian bricklayers built tombs,
temples, and homes from stone and
bricks made of mud.  What kind of
work did other Egyptians do?

## Classes

Daily life depended on one's class. Slaves lived the harshest lives. They did the worst jobs. Their owners could beat them or even kill them. But not all slaves lived badly. Some families treated their slaves like family. Some even adopted slave children as their own.

**Some Egyptian slaves became skilled in making pots, vases, or clothing.**

Farmers and craftsmen worked hard too. Farmers planted crops. Plows and other tools were used to harvest grains. Craftsmen made pots, clothing, and other goods. These people usually lived in small homes made from mud bricks.

Mud was formed into bricks and then baked in the sun. Modern people in hot, dry climates still build homes out of mud bricks.

Scribes, priests, and nobles led the best lives. They lived in the biggest homes. Scribes ran the government. Priests worked in Egypt's temples. Nobles were the highest class. Among them was Egypt's king, or pharaoh. The pharaoh was even considered a god!

**Egyptian artists honored pharaohs by carving statues of them.**

## Communication

The people of ancient Egypt spoke Egyptian. The language no longer exists. But some Egyptian churches still use a form of it called Coptic.

Egyptians had two main types of writing. Many people knew the simple system of writing called hieratic. This writing looks a little like cursive. Egyptians used it for daily tasks such as recording harvests.

This hieratic writing tells an Egyptian king's account of a battle. It was written on thin paper made from plants.

The writing system of hieroglyphics was more challenging. This style included an alphabet of more than seven hundred different pictures. Scribes trained for years to read and write.

Can you imagine an alphabet with more than seven hundred letters? Egyptian scribes spent years learning all of them.

Egyptians believed the god Anubis weighed people's hearts after they died. A person needed a light heart to go to the afterlife.

## Religion

The Egyptians believed gods controlled life in Egypt. People worshipped these gods. Priests tried to keep the gods happy. Many gods were part human, part animal. Anubis was the god of the dead. He had the body of a human and the head of a jackal. Jackals are wild dogs that live in Africa.

This Egyptian princess's body was mummified.

Ancient Egyptians believed in an afterlife. A dead person's spirit left the body. But it would come back one day. The spirit needed the body in the afterlife. So preserving bodies through mummification was important.

The Egyptians put oils and beeswax on bodies before wrapping them. This kept the bodies from rotting. Then Egyptians buried the mummies in tombs.

Egyptian tombs were decorated with paintings and sculptures. Historians study this artwork to learn about Egyptian life.

Tombs could be big or small. The biggest was the Great Pyramid of Giza. A tomb held the body and everything the dead person might need in the afterlife. That included gold, artwork, and everyday items.

Some tombs were built with a special room. This room held the things a person would need in the afterlife.

# Chapter 3

# THE CULTURE OF ANCIENT EGYPT

Ancient Egypt had a rich culture. Egyptians developed unusual styles of art. They painted. They sculpted images from stone. Music probably filled Egypt's streets. Tombs and other buildings towered over the desert sands.

The pyramids were built as burial places for Egyptian pharaohs. What else was in these tombs?

# Artwork

Most Egyptian tombs were filled with art. Drawings and paintings were most common. Many of these showed pharaohs or gods. People were almost always shown from the side. The most important person in a painting was always the largest.

Egyptian gods were often drawn as humans with animal heads.

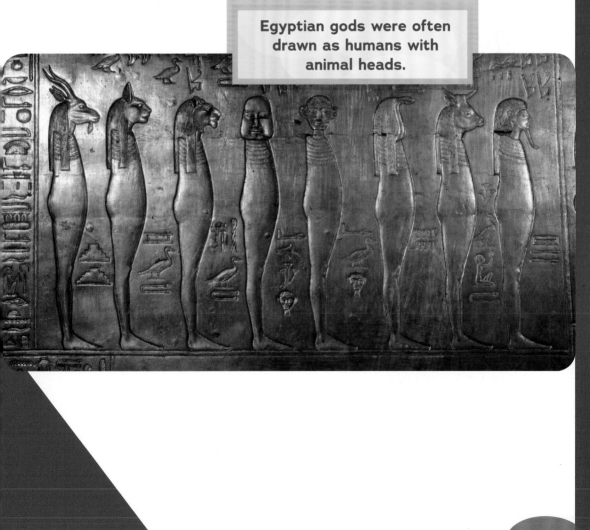

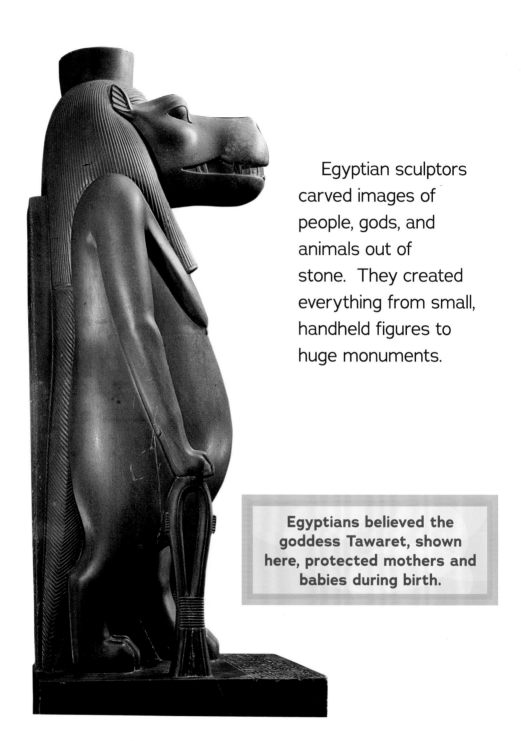

Egyptian sculptors carved images of people, gods, and animals out of stone. They created everything from small, handheld figures to huge monuments.

Egyptians believed the goddess Tawaret, shown here, protected mothers and babies during birth.

Egypt's most famous monument is the Great Sphinx of Giza. This statue shows a creature with the body of a lion and the head of a person.

The Great Sphinx is believed to be more than forty-five hundred years old. This stone statue is 66 feet (20 meters) tall!

These Egyptian musicians
are playing a harp (LEFT)
and a lute (RIGHT).

The Egyptians created many more types of art.
The wealthy wore fine gold jewelry. Potters made fine
pottery. Musicians played bells, trumpets, and stringed
instruments. Dancers moved to the music.

# Architecture

Egypt has no forests. So the Egyptians did not build with wood. They built homes and most other buildings with bricks made of sunbaked mud.

**Mud homes could stay cool even in the desert heat.**

The Egyptians used stone to build most tombs and temples. Egyptian architecture showed their knowledge of math and astronomy. Many temples were built to face the sun or other objects in the sky.

Egyptians often built temples with stars or groups of stars in mind. This temple faced the sun.

The Great Pyramid of Giza was a huge tomb. It stood more than 480 feet (146 m) high when it was built around 2560 BCE. It was built of more than 2 million huge limestone blocks. Workers had to cut, move, and place every one!

THIS PAINTING SHOWS WORKERS BUILDING THE GREAT PYRAMID. THE PYRAMID MAY HAVE TAKEN MORE THAN THIRTY YEARS TO BUILD!

The Great Pyramid was built as a tomb for Pharaoh Khufu. It is as tall as a forty-eight-story building!

The Great Pyramid remained the tallest human-made structure in the world for almost four thousand years. And it's still standing!

## Pastimes

Egyptians probably enjoyed art and music in their spare time. They attended religious festivals. They played games too. A board game called senet was popular. No one knows exactly how the game worked. But senet boards have been found in tombs. Scientists have also found pictures of people playing the game.

Senet may have been like the modern-day game of backgammon. This senet board is more than three thousand years old.

Some ancient Egyptians kept pets. Cats and dogs were the most common. Cats were especially important. Cats were useful to Egyptian society. They caught mice and snakes. Cats also had close relationships with their owners.

The Egyptians thought cats were like gods. Some owners even mummified their dead cats!

**This cat statue is made of bronze.**

## The Journey of Ra

The ancient Egyptians told of the journey of Ra, the sun god.  The story represents life and death.

Ra, the sun, rises every morning in the east.  He swallows all the other gods.  Ra grows stronger as he climbs higher in the sky.  He brings life to Earth and everything on it.  Ra has his greatest power at noon.  Then he begins to dip in the sky.  He grows older and weaker.

At sunset, Ra spits out the other gods.  They become stars.  Ra goes under Earth into the Duat, a realm of the gods and the dead.  But Ra always returns the next morning to bring life to Earth.

Chapter 4

# THE END OF AN ERA

It's hard to say exactly when ancient Egypt began and ended. Its culture developed long before pharaohs joined Upper and Lower Egypt.

Alexander the Great, a conqueror from Greece, ruled Egypt as a pharaoh. When did Alexander the Great take over Egypt?

32

Egypt faced a series of attacks beginning in the 700s BCE. Alexander the Great of Greece conquered Egypt in 332 BCE. Some historians mark this as the end of the Egyptian civilization.

Alexander founded the Egyptian city of Alexandria. The city's library became famous for its collection of writings from many nations.

But the Greeks kept much of Egypt's culture the same. They ruled as pharaohs. In some ways, the civilization lived on. That's why others point to 30 BCE as the end. That's when the Roman Empire conquered Egypt. The Romans wiped out much of Egypt's religion and culture. The civilization that had existed for so long was truly dead.

Greeks ruled Egypt for about three hundred years. This artwork shows Romans greeting a Greek queen in Egypt. The Romans took over in 30 BCE.

Though much has changed in Egypt, the Nile is still an important river.

# Egypt Today

Descendants of ancient Egyptians still live along the Nile. Modern-day Egypt is home to more than 80 million people. The old ways are mostly gone. There are no more pharaohs. The old gods are largely forgotten. Most modern Egyptians follow the religion of Islam.

People worldwide are still fascinated by ancient Egypt. Many visit sites such as the Great Sphinx and the Great Pyramid. Visitors stand in the same locations the ancient Egyptians did thousands of years ago.

YOU CAN STILL VISIT MANY
ANCIENT TREASURES IN EGYPT.

Scientists who study ancient Egypt are called Egyptologists. Egyptologists search for and study art and objects from this long-dead civilization. Every discovery they make sheds a little more light on Egyptian life. Their findings teach us about one of the greatest civilizations in human history.

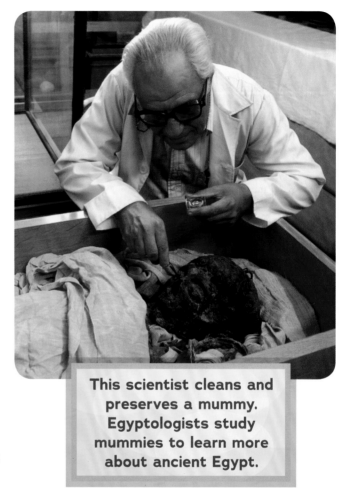

This scientist cleans and preserves a mummy. Egyptologists study mummies to learn more about ancient Egypt.

# Glossary

**afterlife:** a life after death

**civilization:** a large society in which people share a common government and culture

**Egyptologist:** a scientist who studies ancient Egypt

**hieroglyphics:** an Egyptian system of writing that used hundreds of pictures or symbols

**irrigate:** to water a crop

**monument:** a statue or other structure built to honor a person or event

**mummification:** drying and wrapping a dead body to preserve it from rotting

**pharaoh:** a king of ancient Egypt. The pharaoh was believed to be a god.

**scribe:** an ancient Egyptian who was trained to read and write hieroglyphics

**tomb:** a burial place for the dead

# Learn More about Ancient Egypt

## Books

Hamilton, S. L. *Mummies*. Edina, MN: Abdo Publishing Company, 2011. What's scary about a mummy? Find out in this book about ancient mummies that come back to life!

Malam, John. *The Egyptians*. New York: PowerKids Press, 2011. Take a peek at ancient Egyptian objects, and learn how and why these items were used in day-to-day life.

Woods, Michael, and Mary B. Woods. *Seven Wonders of Ancient Africa*. Minneapolis: Twenty-First Century Books, 2009. Visit seven amazing human-built monuments, including the Great Sphinx of Giza, on this exciting journey to ancient Africa.

## Websites

**The Children's University of Manchester: Explore Ancient Egypt**
http://www.childrensuniversity.manchester.ac.uk/interactives/history/egypt/egyptianmap
Discover exciting Egyptian treasures on this interactive journey across historical Egyptian landmarks.

**National Geographic Kids: Ancient Egypt Photos**
http://kids.nationalgeographic.com/kids/photos/ancient-egypt
View photographs of ancient Egyptian works of art, including statues and paintings.

**PBS *NOVA*: Explore Ancient Egypt**
http://www.pbs.org/wgbh/nova/ancient/explore-ancient-egypt.html
Want to walk around the Sphinx? Interested in climbing into the Great Pyramid? Check out this interactive photo site that lets you see ancient Egypt from all angles.

LERNER

SOURCE™

Expand learning beyond the printed book. Download free, complementary educational resources for this book from our website, www.lerneresource.com.

# Index

# Photo Acknowledgments

The images in this book are used with the permission of: © John R. Kreul/Independent Picture Service, pp. 4, 25; © Leemage/UIG via Getty Images, p. 5; © iStockphoto.com/Richmatts, p. 6; © Werner Forman/Universal Images Group/Getty Images, pp. 7, 18, 21, 22, 24, 29; © Tim De Boeck/Dreamstime.com, p. 8; © Laura Westlund/Independent Picture Service, p.9; © The Metropolitan Museum of Art, Rogers Fund, 1930 (30.4.77)/Image © The Metropolitan Museum of Art/Source: Art Resource, p. 10; © Erich Lessing/Art Resource, NY, p. 11; © Mike P. Shepherd/Alamy, p. 12; © Neil Pope/Dreamstime.com, p. 13; © Louvre, Paris/The Bridgeman Art Library, p. 14; © kravka/Alamy, p. 15; © Album/Superstock, p. 16; © Universal History Archive/Getty Images, p. 17; © DEA PICTURE LIBRARY/De Agostini/Getty Images, p. 19; © DEA/G. DAGLI ORTI/De Agostini/Getty Images, pp. 20, 31 (bottom); © iStockphoto.com/chudesign, p. 23; © EastVillage Images/Shutterstock.com, p. 26; © NGS Image Collection/The Art Archive at Art Resource, NY, p. 27; © iStockphoto.com/micheldenijs, p. 28; © DEA/A. JEMOLO/De Agostini/Getty Images, p. 30; © Richard Nowitz/Digital Vision/Getty Images, p. 31 (top); © Gianni Dagli Orti/The Art Archive at Art Resource, NY, p. 32; akg-images/Newscom, p. 33; © North Wind Picture Archives/Alamy, p. 34; © Wisconsinart/Dreamstime.com, p. 35; © iStockphoto.com/karimhesham, p. 36; © Patrick Landmann/Getty Images, p. 37.

Front Cover: © Richard Nowitz/Digital Vision/Getty Images.

Main body text set in Adrianna Regular 14/20
Typeface provided by Chank